HEY FATMAN

For Lucy

HEY FATMAN

Robert Minhinnick

SEREN

U.S. DISTRIBUTOR
DUFOUR EDITIONS
CHESTER SPRINGS,
PA 19425-0007
(610) 458-5005

SEREN
is the book imprint of
Poetry Wales Press Ltd.
Andmar House, Tondu Road
Bridgend, Mid Glamorgan
Wales CF31 4LJ

© Robert Minhinnick, 1994

ISBN: 1-85411-110-9

*The publisher acknowledges the financial assistance of the
Welsh Arts Council.*

Printed by WBC, Bridgend.

Cover image by Geoff Davies.

CONTENTS

Also by Robert Minhinnick

Poetry

A Thread in the Maze
Native Ground
Life Sentences
The Dinosaur Park
The Looters

Essays

Watching the Fire Eater
A Postcard Home

The Swift

The hall is cold, the stairwell dark,
And in my hand the brandy glass
Warm as a child's brow.
I answer the eleventh ring
And hear my question, furred with wine,
Its tiny echo fading like
A lightbulb's filament.

This is the sound the radio makes
When the anthem is played at midnight
And then engulfed by the inaudible
Electric breath between stars.
There's no-one there, no human voice
Describing why it telephones
At this desperate hour for telephones.

But I sit with my hot disc
Of liquor and listen to the fever
Of static, the racing brain-code
Of it that listens to me, and notices
The quickening pulse in my temple
Where the telephone is pressed,
The prickling of my hair.

And I overhear my car outside
Cooling like the brush of moths
Against a shade. This is the voice
Of dust that settles on its empire,
The sound that left my hand tonight
When I picked the swift,
Like a fallen evening-glove,

Dying from the road,
And spread its black crescent
Upon my palm. The weight of a glass.
But now the air tightens
To a strait-jacket around the heart,
And three words like maroons explode
Hard inside the ear.

Are
They ask. And hugely wait.
    You
— A Saharan interval.
       Happy?
And there's a desert in that voice
Come to me from the end of the world.
Now the brandy's hot as a test-tube,
Its perfume clotting in my throat,
And slapping the wall this hand can't find the switch.

The Caretaker's Story

She laughs as she tells it
But I saw she was afraid.
I have heard this woman scream
At a footfall, known her sleep
Disturbed by a moth in a bedside glass.

The vestry light hung from its rose
On a disintegrating cord.
After the bulb came on
You could see the dust
Leaping from its shoulders. White static.

Somehow, it was never cleaned.
But this evening with her pail
And brushes, she was giving
The chapel its Saturday lick
When she glimpsed a shape behind the door.

I can see the widening surge
Of her water across the polished blocks,
Feel her soul tremble
Like a lightbulb's filament.
Yet all it was, she laughed,

Was the minister's robe
For baptisms, a heavy waterproof
Apron. Think of an anaesthetist,
A spotless abattoir gown.
And there below the dripping hem

Were the two galoshes he wore,
One standing straight, the other
Fallen, its shining mouth agape:
His jackboots, as he called them,
For wading into the tank.

Today had been especially good.
Five immersions, and all
Brave girls, each with a forced grin
As they stepped in their shifts
As green and coarse as maidenhair,

Off the stone and into that square
Bath it had taken hours to fill.
And there on his arm he held them,
Bare legs against the rubber boots,
Before they were lowered, eyes screwed,

Knees bent, for the long moment
Under the surface, the water
Brief as a moth's wing over the light,
Its bright moustache
Soon vanishing from their compliant smiles.

Homework

The paper comes off in wet
Streamers, and soon we are down
To the hard plaster, green
And pitted as avocado rind.

Outside, they are building
A temple, their nest a papier-mâché
Face that peers down at us
Through the laburnum's dome of flowers.

We thought it was the perfume
That brought such fever,
The bush a shivering lantern
Of wings, and a scarf of petals

In the gutter below. We sat
Beneath it with magazines,
Tired of the tearing work
Of household archaeology,

Revealing provinces of floral print
And a gothic continent.
And as we ripped, so they returned,
Each time with a wasp-jaw of shining mortar,

Labourers on the wing, the wasp-traffic
Building a swarm-house.
Now how much like a heart it hangs,
Chambered, fiercely beating

With the season's old compulsion.
I'll let it swing there in the fork
Drying like a garlic-bulb
Till winter strips it skin from ruined skin.

Harriet

There were Christmas cards and cups of tea
But after an hour of the class
I knew I was losing them.

Six faces, December-pale, had begun
To glance outside at a day
That had never really started.

The sky was like the cratered asphalt yard
Where the caretaker now laboured
With a delivery of smokeless fuel.

"Why don't we try something new?"
She whispered, the almost pretty one,
The one with a gold tooth and a physics degree.

Odd, but everyone seemed to know
At once exactly what she meant.
They brought a glass from the kitchen,

Cut a crude paper alphabet,
Then dragged the desks together for our board.
And there was my finger on the glass,

Touching, as if feeling for a pulse,
My dry forefinger, beckoning,
On the tumbler's thick green hull.

O spirits, I thought, in whom I do not
Yet believe, how we must bore you
With this inquisition. And why, o phantoms,

Should you bother with our words?
But the glass grew warm and slowly
Began to tremble on the board.

"You see," said a blue-haired grandmother,
Eerily matter-of-fact, "we have called a presence down
And it must do as we bid."

Our time was up. We should have left it there.
But the graduate was not content.
She asked our visitor to name itself,

And this time the glass shimmied like mercury,
Then seemed to float above the desk,
Surely unimpelled by our light touch.

I saw the science die in both her eyes,
The powder on her face stand up, erect
As frost. And she was out across the yard,

Her Metro gunned towards the town
Before we understood the spelled out word:
Harriet: the name of her dead child.
The envelopes lay ripped beside her chair.

Harry Allen Speaks from his Nursing Home

There's a choice of breakfast egg,
Perhaps a visitor in the week,
And when I sleep I never dream,
Everything's completely black.

It's years, but I can feel my hand
On the lever, smooth as the easel-peg
You squeeze when giving blood.
Dying? People in this place beg

For it, like another medicine,
The last promise. There's more mystery
In a soap-opera. Those duties
Offered a career that kept me

Comfortable. I did an exact job
Like any good engineer;
Finished my homework, was always
Well prepared. Knew enough to care,

But not to worry. And all I hope
Is that someone is as business-like
With me. Remember, it was a profession
With its own pride. The state's shrike,

You'd call me; I'd rather think
It a matter of hygiene:
One of the back-room boys you never see
But depend on to keep things clean.

What the documentaries say
Is wrong. I'll never believe
Any were innocent. If there's a fault
It's that putting people away for life

Doesn't mean what it says.
Take Donald Nilsen, the bachelor-
Type, writing poetry with five young boys
Green as candles under his floor,

Wrapped in blankets and odour-eaters.
He stuffed them in a bonfire
That burned all night. I'd have volunteered
To put that man away, but we prefer

To do it differently now. Okay,
It's not the law we put on trial,
But even I choke on some things:
Like Brady talking to that little girl

And his blonde piece recording it.
I didn't listen but there's plenty do:
You can buy the tape in Manchester
Or one of those downstairs shops in Soho,

There's even photographs, before,
After. My paper every summer's
Full of it. Anyone who drives on
The M62, passing that red concrete rose,

Then the white, can see where it happened:
But the grave's invisible, or just
A mark in the grass like a hare's form.
Thank God the TV won't let us forget.

So I ask, what's the point of it?
Like me they're simply paying dues
And waiting to die. It's the last stop on the road
And what we've learned is now no use,

At least not to ourselves.
We all stand in the London Dungeon,
Waxworks behind glass, schoolchildren
Disappointed if the video isn't on.

But if you can't imagine being me,
Too bad. There's some here get the shivers.
It's like that nature programme asked:
What would the world be like without spiders?

The Vietnam

February's colour is concrete:
On the precinct it is always February.

Too far gone to worry about us
A redwing in the subway

Hunches into the gutter, the rain
Or snow, like key-cutter's swarf,

Hanging under the lamps.
In suspended time we seek any refuge —

This one is The Vietnam, with its dado
Of hard faces, and couples that cling

To one another like a final
Absolution. All the city's misshapes.

Careful now. The weak lightbulbs
Are x-ray machines, these tabletops

Confessionals. Black furrows of cigarette burns
Are the ogham of an earlier race

Disturbing our singularity
With evidence of better claims

To the wisdom here, the genius
Behind all its assumptions.

The first task is to use our eyes.
At this table someone's surpliced glass

Speaks a monumental absence;
A dart's bronze torso rolls upon the floor,

Its dimpled barrel weighty, surprising
As a foreign currency.

So easy to miss the vital signs
In all the banality of looking.

Yet that brute who aims the arrow
Knows delicacy. Watch him replace

The flight, violet, petal-fine
As gently as ringing a bird's leg,

And hold, points down, the fletched triumvirate,
Like a small bouquet. Poised now, tiptoed

On a margin rubbed invisible,
He squints into the future, makes it his.

Archaeology

He lies where
He buried himself,

Bones laid out like a toolset,
Ratchets, broken levers,
All smeared the colour of starlight.

He swam, he flew.
He kicked the moon's dust
Into a typhoon;

Stole a piece of the sun
And burned himself,

Sent the tides backwards
And made the rivers flow uphill.

They say he ran shouting
From his house with his hair on fire,

A madman
Who forgot his own name.

Return to the Court

Every ten paces I turn to look
For his crooked silhouette in the rock,
That profile I might recognise

In the hawthorn's stoop, beyond
The frost flashing like a cycle's spokes.
But stepping back into the shade

He eludes me, and I return to the court
Where the single fruit is an oaktree's gall
High against the light like a black planet.

Yet the year has ceased its long descent.
The buds of the snowdrops are fine
As needles' eyes, and a tumour

Of moss swells each node of the elder.
But I was here when the iron
Of the range was sweet with bread,

And the comfrey under the hedge
Stared back like a classroom of blue eyes.
I was here before the mortar turned to ash.

Now, only water is unbetrayed,
Falling in its familiar scythes
From the ice-edged pool into the stream

Where a black reflection on a black surface
Is his shadow, moving towards the turmoil
Of our mingling, where the current

Thrashes under the wheel, and panic's taste
Is the dropwort leaf, the civet-strong iris,
As I balance over the flow.

Meanwhile, on a shelf upstairs,
The pigeons leave the year's first eggs
Like two white cinders growing cool.

Daisy at the Court

"Arithmetic and manners, start with those":
And he had left her on the stair
And gone off after partridges, small bundles
Of feathers you'd tread on before they'd move.

So this was it. A house as long as a street,
Stone lions, and the Welsh language
In a shield on the portico. One of the children
Already pawed the darkness under her skirt.

In a newspaper once she had wondered
At the Cherokee leader who claimed
The worst part of exile was having nowhere
To bury your dead. "Yes", she murmured,

Picturing homesickness as a white
Lily, one of those flowers grown
For the graveside, a field of lilies
Whose perfume was a secret shared only by herself.

"This isn't home", breathed the nanny, a girl
Whom no child had sucked, thinking of
The charcoal ovens in Dean, no bigger
Than beehives, the warmer vowels:

This was foreign, even the bread was strange,
And at dinner the men came out
Of the greenhouses and looked at you when
Your back was turned. Especially the ones with wives.

And yet. There was Ivor, most often Ive,
(Christian names in this country split in half)
Who saluted every morning, except once,
When his hands were cupped for her in a nest

Of blond apricots; who had walked her down
To a corner of the long garden,
Where water was spun across terraces,
Looped and stretched over rocks, before falling

Like a roll of silk into a pool.
"This is a palace," he had said. "At Catterick
We slept fifty to the barrack-room
And still the windows froze on the inside:

"In the village we cut the avenue
Of elms, a hundred years old, for firewood;
There's some eat only gooseberries and milk.
But here is a place hard times don't touch."

She had looked at him then and felt
All the ghostly answers of a sum unwritten,
As the Wolseley bit into the drive's gravel
And a man leaped out and strode towards her.

5 Minutes M4

Across the road the sign goes up,
A red *for sale* against the pebbledash,
And we turn away from the window.
People don't stay these days but simply
Leave behind ideas of themselves
In double-glazing, parking-space,
Flower-baskets like dead barbecues.

Two couples in a year, you say:
No children, good cars, but their names
Never registered: rubbed out like cheap paint.
The traffic's made a frontier of the road
And either side is a different country
Looking from watch-towers, fearful of news,
Over hedges sharp and evergreen.

But your smile says something other
Is to blame. You sketch again the wheatstone pub
With its counter hinged like a coffin-lid
And the barrelstopper oozing
A dark crust. Three-foot walls preserved
The inn's airfrost, kept the tavern
Matriarch in woollens until June.

Once in a while a tailor stayed, stitching
Workshirts and coloured petticoats,
A dainty man with a belt of pins
Preaching beery atheism. He stood
His round, but prate like that grew tedious.
So your grandmother knocked the candles out
And shut the bar. The guests groped to their beds.

And here's the pinch. One night at two or three
She heard a scratching at her door
And the tailor's shrill beseeching for her love.
Or so she thought. The beer had been powerful,
Raising meths-blue veins in the drinkers' cheeks
Before she'd sealed the cask. Angry at
His delirium, she kept the bedroom closed.

By dawn she'd sluiced the flags, scattered
A bucket of the hearth's pink ash
Around the rhubarb-patch. No sign of the last lodger,
So she had taken to the tailor's room
A dish of tea. And there was her amorous
Nietzsche, upright as a doll in bed,
And the colour of Irish linen.

A sudden death, but what of it?
That woman had lain out colliers
And bright, tubercular children, light as birds.
Yet it was the tailor's face that snatched the breath,
And for years gave her the authority
Of legend-bearer, hushing a noisy
Tap with this foremost tavern myth.

Fear, she would say. He died of fright.
His lips were drawn over the teeth
As a dog will change from smile to snarl,
The gums drained white. On a chair
His needle-cushion shone in the sunlight,
Every eyelet pierced with a thread.
A block of flannel lay like a side of beef.

Those who follow a godless craft
Find bitterness. That was her instant epitaph.
But your grandmother was no prig.
She peered into the tailor's eyes,
Vitreous as shirt-buttons, for that image
So terrible it had stopped his heart,
As if its shadow might have lingered there.

This was a man who died of what he saw,
But died believing. Of what, you never knew.
There's no-one else I've met has heard of this,
But some cold current in the air
Eventually disturbs the newcomers.
People these days, you say, won't stand for it:
And you smile with a mouth tight-lipped with pins.

The Birdcage

We crowd the landing, staring up
For the second time tonight.
Listening.
Slither of starling feet:
Pointillism of dust:
Water's secret conversation with itself.

My father, no carpenter, saws planks
And nails them over the attic door:
Six inchers, too big for the job,
Silver and cruel as herons' beaks.

We never go up there. Now it is sealed,
An empty room with bags of clothes
And a birdcage still with the grey
Piece of cuttle between the bars,
A red plastic budgerigar
Wired to its trapeze.

But she watches the work until the last
Nail bends, botched, in the timber.
I can tell what she is thinking.
There's no way in:
There's no way out.
So this will settle him, the attic-man,

He of the starling-scrape, pigeon-wheeze,
The mimic of water's slavery
In the pipes. I see him starve in her mind,
Diminish, meek as cuttlefish.

No longer will he press to the eyelet
In the plaster, watching the bath-steam
Rise from green water, or listen
Through the laths to her delirious
Incantation of his name —
The voice of sleep-in-life that never sleeps.

There's nothing for him now but the silence
She would rack him on,
The cracks of moonlight
A snail's trail on the slates.

He is shrinking, her companion,
The thumb-sized lover-enemy
Rocking imperceptibly
In the shadow-quilted cage.

A film of sawdust prints our steps
As we clear shavings, leave behind
The hammer with its dimpled rubber haft.
And while the kettle boils to celebrate,
I help her pull the door's stiff bolts,
Hear our keys chime on their nails like icicles.

World War II Comes to XXI Heol Eglwys

Even without a blackout
There was not much to show.
A street of cottages and whitewashed pub
Well used to the art of dousing
　Every trace of light.

You knew the Heinkel's unique drone —
Big, angry maybug trapped in a shade —
Yet here was one lower, and faltering.

The Swansea bombs were a murmur at dusk
But this was the first you had ever heard fall:
　Thin steam from a kettle;
　The whine of sap in a sycamore;
　Mosquito's itchy piccolo.

Under the table you felt the house's gentle shift,
Making itself more comfortable.
A joist shuddered, perhaps a slate
Escaped its nail.

And the next morning
Stood out in the field staring into the crater
That 500 pounds of German dynamite had dug.

At the rim you found a cow's horn
Polished like the haft of a walking-stick,
And noted the mattresses of roots, silver now,
In the wall of the pit.

"If the buggers could aim", your mother had said,
Shaking the plaster out of the tablecloth,
"They'd be dangerous".

The Telescope

It was the middle of the afternoon
When I looked at the house called Brynhyfryd.
All the front curtains were tightly closed
With the lace browned at the bottom
Where it had trailed the damp sills.

I had always known the people there. No question
Of a holiday or sleeping in,
There was a death in the house
And the curtains with their grimy watermarks
Were its publication.

They were pulled across but I could set the scene.
She would be sitting in the parker-knoll
With her coat tight around her ribs,
And that curious hat, like a turban,
Fluted at the crown, blue as a mussel-shell.

Sitting, they called it, or *coming in to sit* —
A tribal act of respect.
They used to do that once, the women
And some old men, offering themselves
Simply, speechlessly, to the darkened room.

Brynhyfryd was the house my bedroom faced:
Once I saw a planet rise
Through the cloudrace of the night sky
And the rays descend from Venus
Like a broken stair, down to the ridge-tiles.

If the man in the moon is clear as clear
You might see his blue spectacles.
Ha, I thought, mere nursery lore,
But kept the icy barrel of the telescope
Above the roof moss and the grubby lace,

Dipping only in weakness
Into rooms where neighbours sat,
Or stiffly moved through ceremonies
Of fire and china, the inexplicable
Rites of those who think themselves unseen.

For this house too, had briefly swum
Inside the lens, this house shut fast
To the afternoon. So who will want them
Now, I ask, who's left to consider
The poker curved and black as a fernroot,

Or on the mantelpiece that stone
With its fossil perfect as a child's
Footprint: all the abandoned puppet-show?
I look at the house and all I know
Is I saw what I saw, heard what I heard —

If the man in the moon is clear as clear
You might see his blue spectacles.
She had hissed at me and now she sits inside
Rocking, muttering, duty done,
As I walk past the door of Brynhyfryd.

2, Windsor Road

Memory
Is the inheritance
That is always in dispute.
It's also the slipperiest
Deal we get.

I'm okay on the garden
Which was simply lawn,
And, oh, a pool where three mottled carp
Big as magnolia buds
Lay under the braid of weeds.

Indoors it gets harder.
I recall a bookcase stuffed
With the entire H.G. Wells
Between red boards; everything
That is but *The Time Machine,*
Missing, presumed borrowed.

But what's always there,
There, is the sugar-tongs
Polished like a surgeon's instrument.
It's what I looked for first,
Lifting the cubes from the bowl

To build an obelisk,
Then allowing the crystals to slip
Through the talons
As I carefully relaxed my grip,
Into liquid, thick, undrinkable.

from A History of Dunraven

1. The Inheritors

With the headlights off,
The tape turned up to max

The Astra roars in first
Between the warning signs.

From the air the fort's a faint sketching,
Green ammonite in the rock.

There's not a wall, not a ditch
You might point at and say,

Here they persevered, the first ones
In a desperate place, a cliff edge

Mauve with sea-kale, neighboured by
Ghosts and psychopaths, making their stand

On an arrowhead of the cliff,
This limestone buttress, sea-foam

A starry lichen staining its rock.
Was their music solace or the last

Defiant act? That anthem for a better time
Dated them, placing their tryst

In its unarguable context
As they sat, belted in, burned

White, fused to the machine,
Pure as fossils and all the humdrum

Plastics of the shore, and the sea
A disinterested echo, miles out.

2. The Ice Tower

They packed it in straw,
Carried it on paddles to the kitchen,
Were grateful for its constancy.

And in its cellar
Ice comforted itself,
Fed like grief upon its own image.

Ice was master
And mistress in this tower,
Its ridged wall the colour

Of dragonflies, its sweat
Pearling the darkness,
The gutter running as it sloughed

A snakeskin of glacial
Purples, ebb-tide greys.
I listened, said the scullery-maid,

Hurrying down from the castle
One June evening, the gorse
Ecstatic as goldfinches;

And heard the sound it made, a lover's
Groan, something I should not say.
I rushed out to the gate-house

Frightened of a footfall
Not my own. But there was nothing.
Only the tower behind, its door bolted

And my poor hands raw
From where I had sawn the blocks;
No splinters, yet the slow needlework of blood.

3. Temple Bay

No statuary or white marble
But all the same a shrine,
Sabrina's villa in a crook
Of the bay, the gramophone's
Hissing jitterbug, a champagne
Bottle in a glove of frost.

And sometimes, the king himself,
Hilarious, well-wined,
Plunging to the shoulder
In some inscrutable pool,
Or shiggly on a limestone sill
Cruel as razor-wire.

Behind him, the black
Hexagon of the cavemouth
Where the kitchen-girl, nipples budding
Through a beach-dress frilled
Like a sea-anemone, calls him back,
Their picnic danced flat in the sand.

4. Red Data Book

Lists mainly, in shaming Latin.
Epitaphs for next year. Next week.

Of course, there are peoples too
Who might be honoured in its pages:

The Kreen-Akore, the Mandans:
Their stone-age pinioned by cameras.

But of the inhabitants of Dunraven
Only one is named, falco peregrinus,

Gwalch glas, peregrine, the slayer
Of racing fowl, fox of the loft.

I saw Enoch Powell once, tiny,
Squat as a goshawk, shaking

With rage as he described a plot
That had done him down.

The crowd was not prepared to blink. It knew
The danger there like a rank smell of its own.

And every June the peregrines
Quarter the cliff; ultimate ferocity

With nowhere to go. Their beaks
Are tin-openers for the sternum,

Clawgrip an iron-maiden lock.
That sort of purity can't last.

Meanwhile, in the Non-Political,
For the second night, three men spread maps

On a table-top, open a jewellery-box
With a satin base, soft as a bean-pod.

Think of the agate that could nestle there;
The garnets. They dint the fine material,

Prepare a place of honour
For two warm, white stones.

5. A Kind of Jericho

Down in the fruit-garden the children
Were smelling the currant bushes.
"Poultices", said Annie. "Tomcats", smirked the boys,
"Or outside privy after Miss Pritchard
Has come out, smoothing her apron."
"I'm glad I'm not a bee", shrieked Annie, tearing off,
Back to the packing cases, the impossibility of it all.

Every day for a month the square green van
With the gold lettering had edged down
The cliff road, past the gate-house, and then up
The castle ascent. The driver carried
A bottle of tea; his young men had basin-cuts
And talked about the palaver, the malarkey.
No complaints though. This was serious work.

They dropped a mirror, nothing fancy, in the courtyard.
Its abacus of icicles lay
Uncleared all week. That said it all.
Milord was upping sticks, putting lot-numbers
On the centuries. In the laundry-rooms,
As big as any estate farmhouse, they were
Coppering the winding-sheets of Dunraven.

Impossible to say now who got what.
The sets of blue Nantgarw were knocked down
To a hundred collectors. There are thatched
Vale pubs where the silver heads of ibex
Frame the video screens. And when the blizzard
Ceased, everything from the catalogue,
Down to the last cracked po, had disappeared.

Yet this was only treachery's prelude.
What remained was the castle, quoined
On a promontory above an ocean
Chalked by porpoises, hostage to leisure.
A team of quarrymen were hired, who placed
Their dynamite under weight-bearing walls,
Consulted for days on the angles of collapse.

A mile away the crowds could feel the tremor
In their knees, saw a flower of spray
Conceal the house. And when it lifted
There was a hole in the world.
There were some who picked for years over
The moraines of plaster the explosions built.
And some who have cursed a plague-plot.

6. The Last Man

Take this pill, they said.
You will see visions.
Alternatively it will destroy
Any visions you already have.

Bylo gets them in the Club
For the price of a round
And crouches now
Shivering over a caib.

Naked but for cut-offs
And his famished work-boots
With their half-moons of steel
He's white as belly-pork.

I'd send him home
But it's fifteen miles
And he has fifty pence in his pocket.
So he trembles here,

Pupils like the pricks
Of hypodermics,
A buzzard's feather
Behind his ear:

No snap, no flask,
Only that irradiating grin
And the name of his daughter —
Arianwen —

Like something his blade has found
Gleaming in the ruin;
A kind of wealth
Making him dangerous.

Hey Fatman

Me? I was only watching. Nothing else.
It had been one hundred degrees that day
And I'm not used to frying. So I took a seat
Outside and ordered a drink.
The beer came in a glass like a test-tube,
The colour of that monkey, the golden one,
They're trying to save around there,
The one with the mane like a lion.
And Christ, it tasted cold as a dentist's drill.

But after a while I felt the energy
To look around. And I saw
What I expected to see from a street like that:
The last soccer players on the beach,
A big surf pounding, angry, futile
In the place where it always stopped its charge,
And a beggar eating fire,
Walking up and down outside the restaurants,
A magician folding banknotes for his pimp.

At the bar stood the boss in a mildewed tux,
The sweat hanging off him in icicles.
He looked at me once and passed over —
Not important, not a player tonight.
I ordered another to make him doubt,
But he never blinked. You can't buy style.
So I studied his empire's neon sign
Out on the pavement. There was a moth on it
With wings like two South Americas.

It was bigger than my hand. But either
Nobody had seen it or nobody cared.
I wanted to scare it off that scorching globe,
Grab its wings like the old man's black lapels,
But it was impossible to move.
I couldn't get out of my chair,
Couldn't speak. So I sat and looked,
With a radioactive thirst, at the bar
And its imperceptible protocols.

The women were in by now, four of them
At the counter, each holding a drink
With an hibiscus flower in it, and a straw:
One white, one black, two mulatto,
Like my beer. In ones and twos they'd get up
And stroll outside to the pavement,
Amongst the tables, sometimes out of sight,
Wandering around the expense accounts,
As the city's electricity came on.

They weren't collecting for charity,
That's for certain. I couldn't understand
A word, but I knew what their smiles said
As they squeezed past, what their fingernails
Meant as they chimed against glass,
The stick-on ones, red as foxgloves:
Hey fatman, that's what they said;
Almost without saying it, if you know what I mean.
Because that's all it takes in a place like that.

Their earrings said it, their crossed
And uncrossed legs: and off they'd go
With the turks in singlets,
The executives in their button-downs,
Up a darkened stair behind the bar,
And the old man there in opera black
Would smile with his blue iguana lips
As he held the door for them, then pulled it fast,
His armpits dimpled like a garlic-press.

Ten minutes later you'd think there were four
Different girls. No so. The younger ones
Were older now, the brunettes reborn as blondes.
And they'd suck their drinks and circulate,
Trailing a perfume through the room
Of their own sweat, like a herb crushed underfoot.
Hey fatman, it said to the night,
To the brass propellers of the fan
That uttered ceaselessly its quiet scream.

I watched the moth float down like charred paper.
Over the walls the baby roaches ran
Warning of fire, waving their brown arms.
Down through the haloes in my glass
I saw a furnace glow, the table blistering.
A man in the mirror tried to douse his boiling eyes,
But the women of the city combed their hair,
Buckled on silver, strapped on gold,
Then stepped once more out on to its hot coals.

Air Lounge Haiku

Newark

Latest *Rolling Stone,*
Pitcher of Budweiser.
I think I could live here.

Indianapolis

Alligator shoes
Speckled with ketchup.
Pottawatomees' holy ground.

O'Hare

Our eyes must surf
One hundred blue screens.
My flight always the next channel.

Denver

Bourbon round a glacier,
Sodium-free fries.
One mile high and still grounded.

Albuquerque

Outside the desert
Like cigarello ash.
Someone will come for you.

Seattle

Bag straps manacle
Her wrist. Despite the sirens
Sleep has stolen her.

Washington

The carousel takes round
A crimson satchel.
Where is the audience?

Newark

Luggage outside
Moves like a Raj elephant.
The last ticket is torn.

Rio Sul

1.

She has pitched her booth at the tunnel-mouth.
Here the sun slows us down

Like an American meal,
And we sit on the iron slats

Where the soiled petals of banknotes
Blow around our feet

And each lance of the hibiscus
Shakes its rust over our shoulders.

2.

Across this square the candle-seller
Works through the afternoon,

Her bundles of ivory
Built about her like a child's fort.

So many candles today, their flames
Only stone-coloured in daylight,

While the woman stirs chicken-skins
In a sawn-down oil-drum

And her babies lie open-eyed
Like lizards under the stall.

3.

Perhaps we have taken someone's seat.
Swimmers come out of the bay,

Towels at their necks like rosaries,
A pavement family sifts our useless change.

But no-one claims this place
And under the hoardings beside the church

We sit and watch
A scented metamorphosis,

All the genealogies of wax
Radiant between the yucca leaves.

4.

Now here is a candle with a disciple's
Face, considering the square,

A peacock whose blue body
Trails a rick of smoke.

And here is the candle-seller
Under her broken parasol,

Rolling the tallow, trimming the wicks
Black as her children's eyelashes,

The candle-seller heating her stew
On the penitential flame.

The Woman from Los Alamos

The snow in the canyon
Has turned grey as driftwood,
Its touch like my grandmother's hand.

Hair of the cactus
Is a sunburn I carry
On my wrist and fingers
As a memory of the cold,

Whilst my shoes disturb
The indian-file of the ants
Marching with their booty
Towards the pyramids.

I had looked down on this country,
The great squares of the states adobe-red,
And seen the fingerprints of glaciers,
The lakes to the horizon scattered
Like the highway's silver hubcaps.

And now here is its soft earth
Holding rocks that refuse to warm,
The nubs of cacti like threadbare tennis-balls,
And an outcropping of quartz
Curious as a meteorite.

The woman from Los Alamos
Stirs the skillet of the soup,
And a thrush with its breast
Full of holes like the snow,
Explores the syllables of alarm.

"Today," she says, "the bears came down to the orchard
And forgot to close the gate;
I saw crickets on their yellow wings
Bump-starting in the cottonwoods.

"There are two million acres behind this wall,
Give or take a mountain range,
Full of languages that you will never learn.
Go out and speak in yours."

Chemistry

Amongst the gloomy vitriols,
Glass-stoppered, the violet
Then invisible roots of bunsen flames,
She paced her territory.

And thirty pairs of eyes
Would move away from the retorts
And study a dark fan of hair,
The white technician's coat.

I liked the lab, its smell of gas,
The smoking turds of phosphorous
Angry at the air. But especially
The cabinet where our crystals grew,

Those pillars of copper sulphate
Like fungi in the dew,
Up, out of reach, on a high shelf,
A patient man's experiment.

Once at the dishes she had paused
And moved the filter-paper wraps,
All ritual white like christening caps,
That masked the line of bowls.

Now said her eyes, her poised right hand,
And how the whole class craned and pressed
To see what we had made:
A geometry of glass, like thrushes' eggs

Broken in our cups.
On each bench the bunsens hissed,
Abandoned as we pawed each other's backs.
Gently she set the first crucible down.

Homage to Grimly

Of course, it was the toilets
You saw first. Five minutes
Into the big school, your badge
Still stiff and tropically bright,
Bewildered migrant on a winter lawn,
You were frogmarched
Into the hangar of sulphurous latrines,
A place beyond mythology,
And someone forced your head into the bowl.

Later, alone in the commodious
Stables of Armitage Shanks,
You'd bite your lip at this betrayal
And stare at the two words cut
With a compass point into the paint:
Grimly Fiendish. Was it a name
Or the title of the whole experience?

But for seven years you followed him
With his blades and red indelibles
All the way from cave-man Britain
To Desdemona's handkerchief,
Old Grimly, the philosopher-
Delinquent, mapping your route
With a flourish of one free hand.

Algebra was the language
They might speak on Jupiter,
Tech-drawing an assault course for marines,
But even the blond-haired sadist
With the petrified blue eyes,
The one who would incinerate your arm
With a snakebite in the scrum,
Even he couldn't piss it out.

In the hall are shields and silver cups,
Pictures of oafs in tasseled caps,
And neat inventories of the war dead.
Someone's not there, someone who craved
A different kind of fame. Above
The sparkling porcelain
His signature's a brilloed palimpest.
I take a pencil, pick my spot, and write.

Howard

At poison-touch in the schoolyard
You had to hold yourself
Where the poisoner laid his hand.
I was the last to be tracked down,

And Howard fetched me such a ringing clatsh
Across the ear that I watched stars
Swim like the hundreds and thousands
My mother might scatter on a sponge cake.

So clutching a sore temple
I joined the hunt to catch
The only boy in school to bear no mark.
Up the embankment he led the sprint,

Kicking through a drift
Of black-spotted sycamore leaves,
Retreating as we slowly circled round.
After all, this was someone

Who required our arms' length respect.
Wild as a hawk
Was the village verdict
Passed on a jug-eared Lucifer,

An eleven year-old
With freckles as big as rice grains,
Who would march his enemies
The length of the crumbling school wall

Above a church plantation
Turned to wilderness,
The thorns on the briar-arms
Black as flagon shards.

And as we closed I saw him smile
In a face wrinkling like silver paper,
His coif the colour of new rope
Brushing under our outstretched hands

As he raced into truancy's legends
Of river-dumped books, girls
Knocked up, and bus-station
Prescriptions of benzedrine.

The last time he was glimpsed, a lifetime on,
He wore a Persian-blue
Airforce greatcoat, the Picadilly
Neon cruel in his face,

Before stepping, our prisoner,
Too swift for the game,
Into a doorway and vanishing,
Still skilled, it seemed, at making an escape.

Reunion Street

I jump from the step of the moving bus,
Trying that schoolboy trick again.
And touch suspicious ground.
This is a town where the past still waits
Like a mocking class behind the teacher's back.
Too many people here can claim my time;
I might glance into a shop window
And see the reflections go on forever.

Goosebumped, I know there are ghosts about.
And, after thirty years, Gareth, here you are,
Bald and expansive in a cape,
A cape, for God's sake, uncertain now
In the crowd between the taxi office
And the dark corridor of the video arcade
Cheeping like a battery-farm, the half-term kids
Silent at the coffin-shaped machines.

Bald? I feel my own crown thin, find
Sometimes, unbelievably, a silver
Spider's web on a shirt worn for an hour.
But bald as bath-pumice you stand there,
Perhaps a few pale strawberry hairs
All that's left of the auburn fringe I remember,
Your pudding-basin trim, a bristly tonsure
Scary as a fontanelle, apparent even then.

I like the cape, its tent of tweed
Clasped by a thick bronze pin.
Ridiculous, maybe, but I'll admit
The style, the courage it takes to fight
The wrong way up a street of nudging youths
With barbed-wire scalps and toxic-bright baggies.
You stretch their hairsbreadth tolerance:
I like that too. They think you dangerous.

This might be home and yet it's hard to feel
At ease. The library's computerised,
And the old books in a trolley under
Polythene. Can't give them away, Gar,
A whole decade of second division literature
Hardly date-stamped in a job-lot in the rain.
Books die like people, odorous and slow.
I see their pages curling, silver in the flames.

The last time I met you was over chess.
We used a Victorian penny like black glass
As one of the pawns, pushed a dimpled
Thimble for a rook. The talk of boarding-school
Struck me as a simple, clean betrayal.
The other boys were right. Here was a snob
Who'd been to elocution class, whose family's
Politics were bluer than their swimming-pool.

But who cares now? This six foot-something
Heavyweight has the same wise-owlish air
As the boy who urged me kneel to meet
The chilled, subterranean eye
Of a viper coiled beneath zinc sheet,
Stoop to a reef of fungus in the wood,
Each tree girdled by an orange
Scentless aureole our penknives sliced like bread.

They've shut the flicks, that shrieking coop
Where Jason and the Argonauts fought off
The skeletons. The music in the town's
Long gone, and beer is a desperate nourishment.
Perhaps that's why I stand concealed
And watch you swan up Market Street —
Baffled exotic on an ebbing tide —
Scared by the questions you might ask of me.

53

A Bag of Sweets

Snow on the roofs of all the empty homes,
And yours the coldest in the street
This afternoon. Already
There are patterns on the wall

Your thirty middle-tar a day
Could never reach:
Mirrors missing, picture-frames unhooked.
The migration you began is gathering pace.

And now out slides the oak sideboard
With its secret compartment.
How to find it was our first game,
That place we pressed to ease the spring

And in the dark reveal
Keys with broken teeth, your zebra mints
Rustling in their twists,
And a soapstone face with oriental eyes

Squinting from the gloom.
This, you whispered, placing us
In shivering conspiracy,
Our breath a sweet Antarctica,

Is old, and then the drawer would whirr and close,
And the chinaman return
To the oak's anthology
Of unpossessable wonders.

And now, here's me in my good coat,
With the crumpled hymn-sheet pricking in my side,
Following behind that polished box,
And my tyres two long stripes of black
In the mint-sharp snow.

Elegy for Butetown

The Casablanca padlock fills with rust.
Pigeons shuffle the balcony, somnambulent,
Slow as dope-smoke. But there's still
That painted silhouette, a pianist against
An orange moon, crooner in a tux,
As if this was Broadway with the neon scar
Of 125th Street coming up.

You're careful who you look at there.
Harlem's black glacier hangs over
Columbia State, where Dylan once —
A satyr convalescent, traumatised —
Serenaded sophomores in the English block,
Guitar case opened on the lawn like an autopsy.
That fractured voice.

Here, too, the music trailed away.
Inside's a vault with the last night's
Marlboros unswept, glasses of grave-water.
They stamped your hand with purple dye
When you came into this place, a mosque
With turn-tables, Lavern Brown at the bar,
Red Beans and Rice starting to barbecue.

And strange to think of dancing now,
Clutching the bare forearms of strangers —
Girls with a jewellery of tattoos,
Men with tiny waists, feeling the electric
Shrug of those bodies climb the Richter scale.
Some night, that night you came in here,
Silhouetted on the moon, leaping the silence

Between the last note and the bonecrack of applause.
You queued in the bogs' ammonia, reading
The cave-painters, a text from the Koran,
Knew navvy's sweat like an ice-cube
In the ribs. Only to find yourself
In daylight at a front door welded shut,
Your hands so clean you'd think you'd never lived.

The January Studio

Only your cigarette paints today,
Its smoke a vanishing signature.

Colours are frozen inside tubes,
The canvas anonymous as bone.

And something like the model's boredom
But untimetabled, desperate,

Tightens in your chest.
A dish of fruit, the blue carafe

Are challenges impossible to understand
As they move you now to tears.

So pace about this corner where
A long flower called campion

Hung up like green electric flex
Sheds the day's first petal of scorching paint.

Listening to History

It is there again —
Scissors on the grindstone,
Death rattle of an electric bulb.

Somehow it sounds familiar
But I cannot quite remember
When I last heard
The cog so busy on the spindle.

The dusk puts old age
Into my eyes. From this dune
The fields are dirty banknotes,
A biker on the sands
An angry maybug drawing a helix,
And the thousand white faces of the burnet rose
Impassive now, almost bored,
Like a crowd at half-time.

Yet I know it is down there,
Crouched along a pine branch
As flat as a piece of tortoiseshell
And still as the green, fletched cones:

Goat-sucker, night-crow,
Milk-stealer, fern-owl,
Neolithic footprint
Next to the hiking-boot,
Coif of bracken, coral eye,
And the lost voice searching
For the one who might know it in all this din.

The Swimming Lesson

"Out of your depth", the instructor warns,
But a man might drown in a thimble
Is my philosophy. And for a second
I am sublime. Weightless in a cradle.

"Deep breaths", she shouts, and now I taste
Blood and oysters as the sea swallows
Me, its invincible salt rubbed in
As I thrash in the shallows.

"Breathe", she says, "you need to breathe";
But my body is drawn
Taut as a broom-pod before it detonates.
So this is what it feels like to be born,

I think, before the luxury of breath,
To stammer on the brink of real speech.
And face down in the sand I count
The lipsticked Marlboros that paint the beach

Like sea-rocket, the international
Brand-names discarded by the tide.
This is how I learn to save my life,
To doggy-paddle, porpoise-glide

Into the nameless spaces on the map —
Eryngo-blue isthmus, canal
Of starving eels. But lesson over
I still hold to something more predictable.

"Ah, it's not my element", was what
I always said, a poor excuse
From one who read no horoscopes,
But not unwise. I knew what might douse

The sun. And so for thirty years
I side-stepped with a genius
All attempts to make me swim.
School was worst. At the local baths,

Brutalised by chlorine and the guards'
Insolent musculature
I would sit in tropic changing rooms
Clutching a forged letter,

Whilst next-door the baffling shouts of joy
Drowned the mutter of the pipes.
Even the nunks and fatties swam,
The twitching academic types

Excused from outdoor sports, a ridiculous
Stick-insect in borrowed costume
Braved the deep-end's fathom and a half.
I watched the clock, immersed in shame.

Water, of course was not to blame.
I happily trawled the tannin-
Coloured streams for dragonflies'
Barbarous larvae, the sharp sewin

And minnows thin as pine-needles,
Always an inch beyond a fingertip.
Waist-deep in that cold current
I'd not trouble how a simple slip

Could dunk this non-swimmer
— Hydrophobic with a bucket of young trout —
Under the Ffornwg's dark plumage of weed,
And keep him there until the light went out.

Somehow, this was different:
A homage paid to a primitive god.
Swimming itself seemed as ludicrous
As flying; quite alien to the blood.

So for thirty years of foolishness
I kept myself to the dry ground.
I never sought that stream again,
The civil war of water and the land.

Now England's the set for a commercial break.
Ten miles out of London, signs warn
Of deer crossing, and here the forest
Is primaeval, soft with lichen

Strung like bladderwrack. Where the trees end
Is the Jolly Fiddler car-park
And Rod Stewart's Lambourghini,
A scarlet flick-knife in the settling dark.

Under the saloon's low eaves
The drinkers watch the pipistrelles
Ricochet off walls of air, hear Essex
Chime with evensong's electric bells.

A traveller here, I still look twice
At machine-guns worn on airport stairs
And a man guarding rare orchids
With chainleashed rottweilers.

But that's England now, and we have stopped
Amidst its eastern breweries
For pizzas from the microwave
And surly pints with yeast thick in the lees.

The mansion here is short-lease flats,
Plasterboard and flaking gloss
Dividing like a honeycomb
The hall and drawing rooms. A Polish

Caretaker waved at the gate-house
As traffic brought home office-
Staff and counter-clerks from Harlow,
Parking beneath a high cornice

Of gargoyles, next to leaded panes.
Bedsitterland in Borsetshire
Was how my friend described the pile,
But I was only eager to explore.

Carp nudged the lake's candelabrum
Of lilies, the vines lay thick
In nettledust. Yet the pool was perfect,
Brimful in a courtyard of glazed brick

With diving-board and spotless changing-room.
Dragged daily by the caretaker
Its oval shone in starlight
Like a polished ballroom floor.

That's how I see it still, a pool
Immaculate under lunar
Continents. I crouched to stroke that silver —
Like the hymen of a coffee-jar —

And felt no old unease.
Adnam's had seen to that of course,
And several shouts of Breakspear's
Chased by unwanted Scotch.

Salacious midnight drew us on
Towards the unlit mansion-house,
Yet the last idea of the day
Seemed one of genius.

Clothes and shoes lay where they fell,
And naked, done with merriment,
I submitted to the shallows' manacles.
Water handles us like a parent,

With a hard, incomprehensible love.
Stiff in its embrace we gasp
For air, choke on impossible
Explanations. Think to escape

And the way we came is covered
By the same rough tide that holds us;
Hate it, and it pulls tighter, our
Nostrils burning with its phosphorous.

There was nothing in the water now
But blackness. I saw my hand on the surface
As if smoothing out the pages
Of some brand-new atlas,

Hesitant strokes to brush away the dark.
The others were invisible,
The sparks of their swimming extinguished
Somewhere at the frontiers of the pool.

A swan, a lily, both are moored
By fury and tenacity
To life. But seeking their mirage of grace
I found instead an icy

Millimetre of pondwater
Beneath my heel. And clearly in that slow
Capsize, I saw the sisters venture
To the beach, laughing, years ago,

To the sea's nunnery, all raw-boned girls
In sheaths of black and glistening plum,
Embracing the first weak wave.
I walked the bay where they had swam —

A knucklebone behind the town —
And heard again their gentle ribaldry,
Saw hair piled high in alice-bands,
Their sealheads all miraculously dry.

Then a fist of water took me in the throat
And an electric bulb shone all
Its hundred watts against my eyes,
The filament a red tongue inside a skull.

Hearing the silence, I think I cried;
If so, the words sank useless as iron
Into the pool's still sanctuary.
And there I was a boy again

Bent above a shadow on the stream,
Ragged fringe over the face,
Buttocks pale and thin as willow-leaves:
A hunter in a nameless place.

So thirty years of foolishness
Ended as I dragged my body in,
Spitting the pool's astringency
And moonlight like a nettle on the skin.

Acknowledgements

BBC Wales radio and television; *Border Country* (West Midlands Arts); *PBS Anthology I; Pivot; Planet.*